*I write so that I can further discover and
share what I've learned with others.*
Steven Heller, 2021

Published by:
Artmonsky Arts
Flat 1, 27 Henrietta Street
London WC2E 8NA
artmonskyruth@gmail.com
Tel. 07767 820 406

Text © Ruth Artmonsky 2023

ISBN 978-1-9163845-8-3

Designed by:
David Preston Studio
www.davidprestonstudio.com

Printed in Wales by:
Gomer Press
https://gomerprinting.co.uk

My thanks to David Preston
Studio for their enthusiasm and
imaginative book design.

Ruth Artmonsky

PRINTING PEOPLE
PRINTING PEOPLE
PRINTING PEOPLE

A macramé of players in
the revival of British printing
in the twentieth century

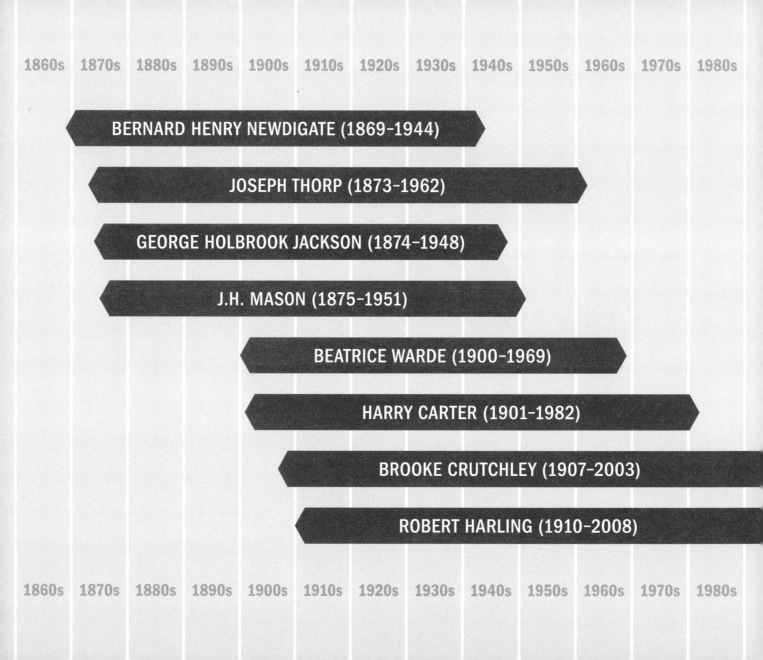

Contents

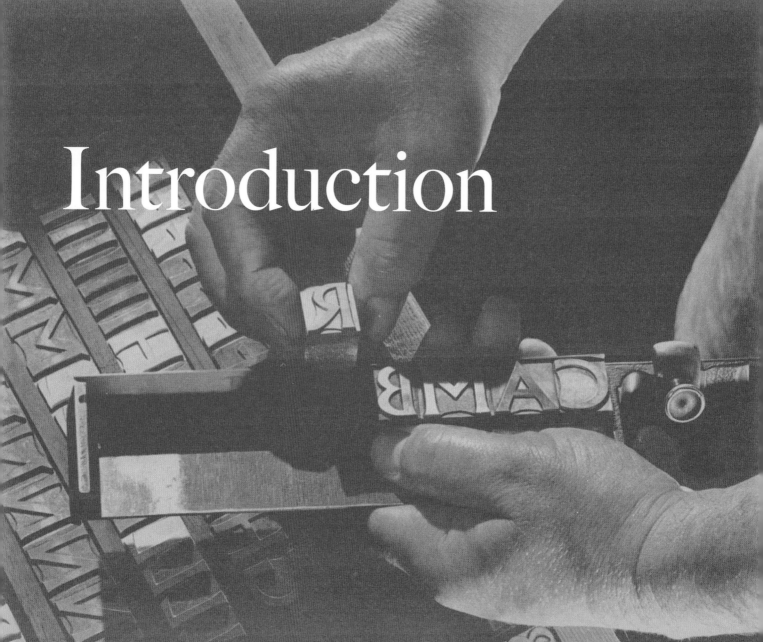

Introduction

What is there about printing which makes such amiable fanatics of us all. Joseph Thorp, 1931

Robert Harling the multi-talented print man, bemoaned the general standards within the print industry after WWII:

> The statement that the allied industries of publishing and printing are responsible for issuing a greater number of different products than any other industry in this century may provoke immediate dissent. The further statement that most of these different products are lamentably – or, at best, indifferently designed may provoke even more violent dissent.

He went on to complain further:

> ...a dozen leading figures with a few score imitators is a niggardly total of responsible designers for a vast industry.

The gauntlet, unknowingly, had been thrown down! A fanatic for lists, I started to jot down who might have been included in Harling's 'a dozen leading figures' and their 'few score imitators'. This did not prove as easy as I thought, but resorting to my own reference books and the ever helpful Google, I managed to build up a list of over thirty names, many of whom, I acknowledged, I knew little about. As is my wont, whenever I find an area of design which arouses my interest and where my ignorance is clear, a possible book comes to mind.

In choosing who from my list to research, I have disregarded the well-documented giants, such as Stanley Morison, Francis Meynell, and Oliver Simon. I have selected eight 'Printing People' I wanted to know more about, chosen because, together, they seem to represent the variety of roles people have chosen to play in relation to printing – archivist, typographer, educator, networker, publicist, and so on. Seeking for a collective noun for my motley crew of eight, as with a coven of witches or a squadron of airmen, I settled on macramé – a pattern of knots – for all of them have threads linking them to the others, either directly or through intermediaries – threads of influence, co-operation, mentoring, joint projects, of friendship. If these relationships were to be charted diagrammatically a wide, complex, irregular knotting would emerge, with threads of different colours, textures and thickness, tightly or loosely secured.

To further the metaphor, within the macramé representing activity in the first half of the twentieth century print world, there would appear three major knots, each with dozens of threads attached to them – the Design & Industries Association (DIA), The Double Crown Club, and the Monotype Corporation Ltd. The Design & Industries Association, founded in 1915, was a group of business people, artists and designers, together flying the banner 'Nothing Need Be Ugly', bent on improving design across all industries. The Double Crown Club (DCC), founded in 1924, was (and is) a dining club focused specifically on standards of design in publishing and printing. The Lanston Monotype Machine Company, founded in 1887, and with a London office by the late 1890s, came to be known here simply as the Monotype Corporation. Initially it pioneered type setting machinery, but it began, gradually, to issue its own type, some of which became the most popular typefaces of the century.

Each of the knots of my macramé of 'Printing People' was linked to at least one of these major knots, some to all three. They were passionate people, some in their own quiet ways, others more rowdily, all crusading for the betterment of all aspects of printing, most devoting their whole working lives to their mission.

Bernard Henry Newdigate

scholar printer

1869–1944

Bernard Henry Newdigate, the most modest, self-effacing of men, would have been embarrassed at the praises heaped upon him by some of his fellow typographers when he died – Stanley Morison considered him 'the most underrated of typographers'; Ruari McLean declared that Newdigate had:

> ...made one of the greatest contributions to the raising of book production standards of the time.

Newdigate was born in Derbyshire, where his father worked as a parish vicar. The family was one of distinction, able to trace its ancestry back to Henry VIII. His father converted to Catholicism, retiring to Leamington and setting up a printing firm. In 1878 Newdigate was consequently dispatched, for his schooling, to a leading Catholic boarding school, Stonyhurst. From there he took what has been recorded vaguely as an 'Arts degree in London'.

Destined for the Civil Service, Newdigate then appears to have taken something like a gap year, travelling in France and Spain, and later dabbling in social work in London. It was at this point that he felt he should return home to help his father salvage his printing firm which was in some financial trouble, which, in its turn, was putting a strain on family finances generally. As a parish clergyman Newdigate's father had printed notices to his parisioners using a gelatin pad. After his conversion, he had met up with a monk, Father Stulto, who was printing Catholic pamphlets at a

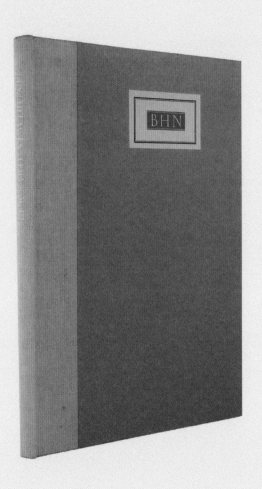

B. H. NEWDIGATE
Scholar-Printer
1869–1944

by
JOSEPH THORP

BASIL BLACKWELL
OXFORD
1950

press in Stratford-on-Avon; Newdigate senior offered to help him in this enterprise. As a result of this collaboration The Art & Book Co. was founded, using the imprint The Arden Press.

In 1890 Newdigate joined his father, and quickly became interested in all aspects of printing – technical, aesthetic and historic. He had been introduced, by an old school friend, Joseph Thorp, to Emery Walker, the typographer running the Dove Press. Walker came to act as a father figure to many young typographers, and, generously, helped the young Newdigate, eager to learn.

Frank Goeby, who was running the technical side of the Newdigate family business, said of Newdigate's early years there:

> I do not feel that I taught Mr. Bernard anything much for he appeared to possess the normal knowledge of a master printer, evidently by study and observation.

Such was Newdigate's passion from the start. Ruari McLean, who, in his turn, worked with Newdigate when he was setting out in his printing career, put it:

> Bernard Newdigate had sprung an almost fully equipped typography from the head of Emery Walker.

The Arden Press mainly carried out Catholic related printing, some commissions coming from the Meynell family's company, Burns & Oates. Of his visits to the Press on behalf of the company and his acquaintance with Newdigate Francis Meynell wrote: 'There I went often, thus becoming both humble pupil and proud patron.'

In 1898 Newdigate senior retired and Newdigate junior was left in charge. Unfortunately his nearly obsessive interest in so many aspects of printing did not extend to financial matters. It was at this stage that his old school friend Thorp reappears. Thorp, frustrated in his career ambition to become a priest, was taken in by Newdigate and set about trying to salvage the business. Thorp was about to get married, and, needing a more assured income, was to join W.H. Smith's printing and publishing empire. He persuaded his friend H.E. Morgan, a Director of Smith's, not only to invest money in the Arden Press but to absorb it. Brownie points to Thorp, and Smith's recorded the Arden Press doing well under its aegis; altogether less satisfied was Newdigate himself. Smith's had told Newdigate baldly that they saw themselves as taking over a business which was not making a profit, that they were not enthusiastic purchasers, and that rewards would depend on tangible results. He felt rudderless in such a large enterprise which he saw as totally lacking his ethics in its style of operating, and his motivation in striving to improve standards of typography.

There followed a career break when, with the onset of WWI, Newdigate enlisted in the Royal Warwickshire Regiment. He was hurt in a motorcycle accident, which resulted in him not seeing action but serving as a musketry instructor. Returning to civilian life Newdigate was somewhat adrift and up pops his old friend Thorp yet again, who proceeded to persuade Harold Curwen, of the Curwen Press, to take Newdigate on. This proved a stop-gap experience for, in 1920, he was fortunate enough to meet Basil Blackwell, who ran both a bookshop and a publishing company in Oxford. The young enthusiastic Blackwell had set up the Shakespeare Head Press and invited Newdigate to join as Managing Director; at last Newdigate was to find his niche.

By temperament and interest the 'managing' aspects did not suit him and these were soon to be taken over by Blackwell and his partners, leaving Newdigate to have the responsibility for the design and printing of books, which was where his true passion lay. He was to remain at the Press for some twenty years. His knowledge of Elizabethan life and literature and his ability to read in both Greek and Latin, resulted in the Press producing works that the American typographer Bruce Rogers rated 'amongst the finest products of the modern revival'.

Whilst with his father's company, Newdigate had come across the typeface Caslon Old Face, which so attracted him that he became masterly in its use. So he was delighted to find the Shakespeare Head Press well stocked with it and many of the books he produced were to be set in it. His exacting standards for the use of type came to irritate the men working in the Press, for even at the proofing stage he could demand that a colon needed replacing with a semi-colon, with a complete disregard for the cost involved, perfection being the aim. Among the Press's limited editions he produced were: *Ovyd, his metamorphoses*, an eight volume Chaucer, Chapman's Homer, and Boccaccio's Decameron. Its standard library editions, priced for general public purchase, included the complete works of those such as Fielding, Defoe, the Brontes and Trollope. In 1935, 50,000 copies of library edition of the one-volume Shakespeare flooded the market.

Newdigate not only influenced by example, by the exceptional standard of the books he produced, but educated via his monthly column 'Book Production Notes' that he wrote for nearly twenty years, from 1920 onwards, for *The London Mercury*, a literary journal that published original work as well as reviews. With few of the skills needed for teaching face-to-face and with an unimpressive stature and high-pitched voice inadequate for public speaking, Newdigate's plethora of ideas on many aspects of

CONTENTS

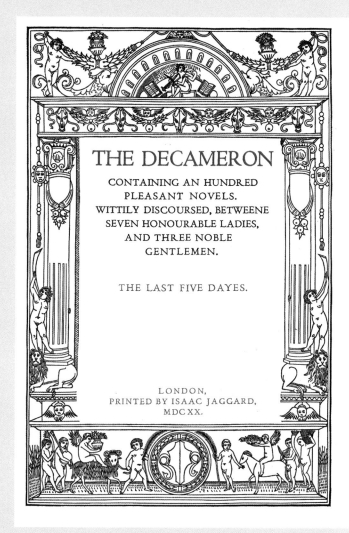

THE DECAMERON

CONTAINING AN HUNDRED
PLEASANT NOVELS.
WITTILY DISCOURSED, BETWEENE
SEVEN HONOURABLE LADIES,
AND THREE NOBLE
GENTLEMEN.

THE LAST FIVE DAYES.

LONDON,
PRINTED BY ISAAC JAGGARD,
MDCXX.

Opposite: Two examples of Newdigate's work at the Shakespeare Head Press.

printing and his ability to communicate on paper, made his column writing an attractive medium for him.

On paper he was forthright, an example being when panning *The Radio Times* with 'paper, type, are all alike bad' and its layout making it difficult 'to find one's way about the daily programmes'; accusing its typeface of 'impairing the eyesight of our generation'. Such was Newdigates' breadth of knowledge and enthusiasms, his notes could be on such varied aspects of printing as the technical qualities of paper or the laying out of verse with the poet's intent in mind.

Particular axes Newdigate was frequently to grind, both in his notes and in articles published in *The Penrose Annual*, Lund Humphries printing journal, were on his strong preference for the hand-set book, and for the importance of compositors to learn calligraphy and hand-writing – both prejudices just blatantly laid down rather than logically argued. In a *Penrose* article in 1933 he wrote:

> Good composition is merely good arrangement of well-designed letters, and the habit of good arrangement is best got by practice of lay-outs which come easily to a good and neat writer but by no means easily to a bad and clumsy one.

The phrase 'physician heal thyself' comes to mind, as his own hand-writing was poor and never improved in spite of his advice to others. In addition to his activities at the Shakespeare Press and for *The London Mercury,* Newdigate worked on three 'specials' for The Studio Ltd. In 1914, *The Art of the Book*, which was edited by the owner of The Studio Ltd. Charles Holme; in 1928, *Modern Book Production*, printed at the Curwen Press; and in 1938 he wrote *and* designed *The Art of the Book*. It was with the last, that the young

17

the art
of the
book

BERNARD
NEWDIGATE

THE ART OF
THE BOOK

BY BERNARD H. NEWDIGATE

LONDON: THE STUDIO LIMITED
44 LEICESTER SQUARE
NEW YORK: STUDIO PUBLICATIONS Inc.
381 FOURTH AVENUE

Ruari McLean worked alongside Newdigate, being allowed to design the case and the jacket.

McLean gives a kindly picture of the aged master at the Shakespeare Head Press – he being an eager beaver, eighteen years old, Newdigate in his late 60s. He described Newdigate as of middle height, with the weather-beaten face and crumpled clothes of an Elizabethan sailor, sitting solitary in his glass-walled sanctuary correcting proofs, whilst beyond compositors worked by hand with outdated presses, the floor strewn with paper. There is no portrait of Newdigate lodged at the National Portrait Gallery, as with some of the others making up the printing macramé, as this modest yet influential printer is said to have been ashamed of some aspect of his chin and banned photographs to be taken of him. On Newdigate's death, Basil Blackwell spoke of his considerable influence at the Double Crown Club and commissioned the biography that Joseph Thorp wrote and Blackwell printed: *A giant among typographers.*

Joseph Thorp

networker

1873–1962

I t was in the early 1920s that a young woman, dusting some 14,000 books in a print library attached to a type foundry in America, took down one of the books, out of curiosity, and claimed that it was at that moment her whole life changed. The book was *Printing for Business*, published in 1919 by one Joseph Thorp; the young girl was Beatrice Warde.

Thorp declared himself to be a late-developer when it came to printing, as he explains:

> I was pitchforked by fate into printing at a mature age than falls to most, and I have learned to bless the folk that pitched me there.

In fact, Thorp was about thirty when he was so pitch-forked. Born in Bath, a son of William Thorp 'gentleman', he grew up in a Catholic household and so was inevitably educated at Stonyhurst and destined for priesthood. However, after some ten years of Jesuit training, it was decided he was unsuited to the calling and he found himself cast adrift with no clear alternative.

It was at this point Thorp remembered an old school friend, Bernard Newdigate, who was working, at that time, in his family's firm, The Art & Book Company (to become the Arden Press). Newdigate, presumably feeling sorry for his old friend, gave him a job in the office. Thorp, now in charge of his fate, soon drifted over to the printing side. He recorded 'My eyes were opened. Here was

Photograph of Eric Gill with Thorp,
by Howard Coster, 1928.

something worth doing'. How much actual formal instruction Thorp received is not at all clear, but he was later to claim to have been one of the first typographers who was not a trained printer. He described his learning experience as 'poking about the machine and composing room'. He perhaps gave a more accurate description in hindsight in 1945: 'after a few months hurried but enthusiastic training under Bernard Newdigate'.

The benefits of Thorp's time at the Arden Press were not at all one-way for it was he, as has been noted, who introduced Newdigate to Emery Walker, consequently widening and enriching Newdigate's work; and Thorp was able to make a contribution to the commercial side of the Press, which was of little interest to the 'detached and almost ethereal Newdigate' as Ruari McLean was to describe him. It was Thorp who was to write an appreciation of Newdigate, his friend of some fifty years, *Bernard Newdigate, Scholar Printer 1969– 1944*, published in 1950.

The Arden Press was in some financial difficulty and Thorp, who had now moved on to W.H. Smith's, began to look for financial backers to help his friend and persuaded Smith's to take over the Arden Press. Thorp, with no false modesty, became self-appointed adviser to the whole W.H. Smith & Sons Ltd. Group – 'writing and designing printing matter' and 'going on the road' to attract more business. He wrote of his time there: 'there was built up out of a dead shop of plodding printers a real fighting organization turning things upside down'.

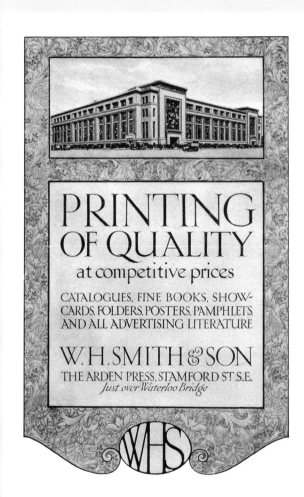

Above: Photograph of Joseph Thorp by Howard Coster.

Right: W.H. Smith publicity poster after their takeover
of the Arden Press, 1922.

DESIGN
IN
MODERN PRINTING

The Year Book of the Design &
Industries Association
1927–28

EDITED
by JOSEPH THORP
WITH AN INTRODUCTION
by SIR LAWRENCE WEAVER

LONDON
ERNEST BENN LIMITED
BOUVERIE HOUSE
FLEET STREET

PRINTING
FOR BUSINESS
A MANUAL *of* PRINTING PRACTICE
IN NON-TECHNICAL IDIOM BY
JOSEPH THORP
PRINTING CONSULTANT TO
W. H. SMITH & SON

MCMXIX
JOHN HOGG
13 PATERNOSTER ROW
LONDON

Title page of *Design in Modern Printing* by Thorp, 1927–28.

Title page of *Printing for Business* by Thorp, 1928.

That Thorp acquired a large social network, which was to prove useful to him, was partly through his membership of the Design & Industries Association (DIA). Thorp had been an active member from its formation and is recorded as being one of the speakers when DIA contributed to an Arts & Crafts Exhibition Society in which it declared its democratic mission –'Nothing need be ugly'.

It was Thorp who wrote the DIA Yearbook for 1927–8, entitling it *Design in Modern Printing*. The book took the form of letters from an amateur of printing to his nephew who was considering it as a career. Although the DIA message permeated the text it exposed many of Thorp's opinions (and prejudices) when it came to printing and to his way of operating in the industry. Writing of a supposed visit the 'amateur' was to have made to a packaging company where the managing director was 'apprehensive lest a lunatic had strayed into his building', Thorp wrote:

> People don't crowd into art galleries: they do passionately consume jam and cocoa, and there is no reason why every cocoa carton and every jam pot should not be a little piece of beauty to enliven difficult lives.

It had been this view, that beauty could be applied to jobbing printing equally as to limited edition fine press books, that had led Thorp to write *Printing for Business*, the book taken down from the shelves by the young Beatrice Warde. In this Thorp stated his opinions in direct non-technical terms:

> In regard to type and type-setting the first desideration is legibility. Decoration is purely subsidiary, and decoration

that jeopardises legibility is just bad workmanship. There is, in fact, no 'high art' nonsense about the suggestion here advanced; it merely amounts to this, that simplicity and dignity and a sense of style will suffice to get a message read more quickly, and attended to more pleasurably than fussy, crowded, over-ornamental work.

'Nicks, twiddles, and daubes and squirms' so admired by the Victorians 'may be condemned out of hand not merely as abominably ugly, and also as utterly inefficient for the job'. He wrote facetiously:

> Should a ruthless committee of Typographical Eugenists ever come to sit solemnly in judgement upon these unfit freaks whose survival can serve no possible useful, not to say beautiful, purpose, I would gladly act as Hon. Secretary and Executioner.

Thorp considered that as an 'amateur' he was best placed to communicate to business people who knew nothing about printing as:

> ...my chief qualification for taking upon me this task is that I really don't know too much about it. The trouble with technical folk is that they do.

The content of the book belied his claim of limited knowledge. Beatrice Warde declared it:

> ...the first book ever written for the man who was not a member of the printing trade – for the business man or the

Cover of the first Curwen advertising booklet created under Thorp's influence.

amateur. It was a clear lucid exploration of printing as a method of communication and as a technique.

One of the most fruitful of Thorp's many DIA relationships was with Harold Curwen. Herbert Simon, in his book on Curwen, described Thorp's influence on him as 'a blood transfusion'. Although it is possible that it was Curwen who invited Thorp to act as adviser to his printing company, given Thorp's temperament and style of operating, it is rather more likely that he proffered his services himself. In fact, the Curwen Press only came to adopt that name on the arrival of Thorp; and it was he whom persuaded Curwen to acquire a printer's device or trademark in the form of a unicorn – a mythical beast known to be a hard fighter. Herbert Simon noted this to be appropriate, as Curwen planned to produce 'courageous and forceful printing' from his Press. Thorp, yet again dipping back into his school days, commissioned one of his fellow students, Paul Woodroffe, to produce the first image of the Curwen unicorn. Thorp, as it were, strengthened Curwen's backbone for the battles ahead; he lent him his oftimes unwarranted but nevertheless motivating optimism; and was able to communicate Curwen's ideas in his brilliant colourful manner in comparison to Curwen's modest rather flat drone. Simon described Thorp's lecturing style:

He's like a prize fighter. You get a blow in the solar plexus, then before you can recover your wind you get a knock out, which leaves you dazed and gasping.

Like a showman he invited recipients of his publicity for Curwen to contact Curwen direct if they felt he was 'getting into a groove'; but went on to declare: 'I shall have done so first! That being part of my job.' Of his work for Curwen, Thorp wrote:

> One of the queer things about the director of the Curwen Press is his pose that he needs my help and advice. Well, I'm glad he is under this illusion.

Although Thorp's attempt to get Newdigate installed at the Curwen Press was short-lived, an altogether more successful linking was his introduction of Oliver Simon. The link was tortuous – Thorp was a friend of the artist Lovat Fraser who was approached by a friend of his, the artist Albert Rutherston for advice on a possible career for Rutherston's nephew Oliver Simon. Lovat Fraser told him that Thorp was the man to help and, in the twinkling of an eye, young Simon joined the Curwen Press in 1920. The rest is history. Once Simon was established, Thorp felt he had contributed all he could to the Press and decided to move on.

Perhaps, as a footnote to this, should be mentioned Thorp's Decoy Press. In fact Thorp never had his own Press – no buildings, no machinery and the only part-time employee, Thorp himself. It was merely a name he adopted when something of his was being printed at the Curwen Press's Plaistow works that might have been ill-advised to go out under the Curwen name. One such was a radical publication called *Change: the beginning of a chapter in twelve volumes*, which argued for a new order based on socialist and religious principles. In the only volume actually produced its sermonizing on the sins of materialism did not sit well with Thorp's own life style – married in St. George's Church, Hanover Square, living in a grand parade of new flats by Battersea Park, a member of the Athenaeum, dandy like outfits, forever in financial difficulties, extravagance leading to several bankruptcies.

Joseph Thorp's own 'press' mark, wood engraving by Eric Gill.

Thorp's strengths were his psychological energy, his persuasive influence, his sociability resulting in a network which was used to his advantage as well as to the advantage of others, an ability to make things happen – and, not least, an evangelical commitment to improving standards of printing – whether 'fine' or 'jobbing'. Holbrook Jackson summarised this:

> Joseph Thorp had been carrying out a war of his own in favour of better lettering and printing. It was guerilla warfare and Thorp, then as now an intellectual franc-tireur, went about letting off squib-like criticism, propounding explosive propositions, and throwing admonitory bombs into the camp of the Amalekites, in the hope of startling some of the more capable of the backsliders into typographical decency.

After the Curwen episode, Thorp went on to work as design adviser to other organisations, including the *Morning Post* and *The Daily Telegraph*, boasting that the printing changes he made with these were copied by *The Manchester Guardian*; in addition, he built up a considerable career for himself as theatre critic for *Punch*. Thorp was a character, an eccentric, an influencer, who, amongst his many activities, unknowingly, brought Beatrice Warde to England and to the Monotype Corporation.

Joseph Thorp with Beatrice Warde.

George Holbrook Jackson

typophile

1874–1948

At the turn of the century, a young man in his twenties, left Liverpool to seek his fortune in Leeds, not long afterwards forsaking both cities to reside for the rest of his life in London. Yet some forty years after settling there both Leeds and Liverpool came to claim him as one of their own and to mourn his death accordingly. *The Liverpool Echo* wrote:

> He was one of the greatest living authorities on books and every aspect of reading and for nearly fifty years maintained an output of scholarly works.

The Leeds Evening Post recorded of his relatively short time there: '[he was] one of the two men who in the first decade of this century, woke up the intellectual and artistic life of Leeds'.

George Holbrook Jackson was born in Liverpool in what he described as 'a poor background'. He left school and took a job as a clerk, but had then moved on to Leeds as an 'agent', presumably a 'salesman' for a textile company. Although with a limited formal education, Jackson was, from an early age, an avid reader and by his teens was trying his hand at writing. It was this literary bent that one day, in Leeds, took him to a local bookshop where he had a casual encounter with a young Leeds teacher, working in the slums, one Alfred Richard Orage. Both young men were interested in left-wing politics, Holbrook Jackson already a member of the Fabian Society, Orage a member of the Independent Labour Party.

Above: Photograph of Holbrook Jackson, by Howard Coster, 1930s.

Right: Holbrook Jackson on the demise of The Fleuron Society in a letter to Oliver Simon, 1922.

At the FLEURON
10 Adam Street, Adelphi, w.c.

26th September 1922.

Oliver J. Simon Esq.,
The Curwen Press,
Plaistow, E.13.

Dear Simon,

      Thanks for yours of the 19th.
I have spoken to Morison and he agrees with you
and me that The Fleuron Society has petered out,
and I think there is nothing more to be done than
to admit this. There has been no expenditure
save the printing of the paper on which this
letter is typed and I have asked Morison to
supply the amount due from each of us, which
will only be a few shillings. The only subscriptions
paid were Morison's and my own. The requests for
subscriptions from other members did not develop
into cheques. I am therefore returning Morison
his cheque. Mr. Newdigate has never answered
any of my letters so I imagine he never considered
himself a member.

    Yours sincerely,

Holbrook Jackson

HJ/GB.

HOLBROOK JACKSON (*Editor of To-day*), FRANCIS MEYNELL (*Pelican Press*)
STANLEY MORISON (*Cloister Press*), B. H. NEWDIGATE (*Shakespeare Head Press*)
OLIVER J. SIMON (*Curwen Press*)

Noteheading: the only document printed by The Fleuron Society

32

A casual interchange in a bookshop started a friendship which Holbrook Jackson called 'a conversation that was to last for the next ten years' – a friendship that took on a cause. Both considered Leeds a cultural desert, given over to grubby commercialism, and decided to start a club to encourage the arts, along with radical thinking. The Leeds Art Club, that was to meet weekly, flourished and soon was being addressed by such dignitaries as G.B. Shaw, G.K. Chesterton and H.G. Wells (Holbrook Jackson was to write one of the first books on Shaw).

By 1906 the two decided to go to London, and by 1907, with the help of funding by Shaw, had bought a struggling socialist magazine *The New Age*, becoming initially its joint editors, working to transform it into a more general arts journal. But then the pair split (presumably on Orage's wife leaving him for Holbrook Jackson). He then took on another editorial role with T.P. O'Connor, an Irish politician who ran a newspaper with a literary bias *T.P.O.'s Weekly*. By 1917 Holbrook Jackson had bought it and converted it into *To-Day*, which ran for some half a dozen years. From then on he appears to have centred his career on journalism and book writing, working on some twenty right up to his death in 1948.

It was in his writing, both of books and articles, that Holbrook Jackson was able to express his ideas on printing which were to earn him his reputation as a kind of guru on the subject. His articles appeared in numerous publications as *The Fleuron*, *Signature*, *The Listener*, *The Curwen's News Letter* and *The American Book Collector*.

His books can perhaps be split into two groups – one on the reading and collecting of books, the other on typography and the designing and printing of books. The former is possibly the larger containing such titles as *The Anatomy of Bibliomania* and *The Bibliophile Almanac*. Even to the years running up to his death the subject was further pursued with *The Reading of Books*, *The Hunting of Books* and *The Pleasure of Reading*.

But Holbrook Jackson, besides being a collector of books, became increasingly interested in their printing, and his articles and books began to focus on the actual design and production

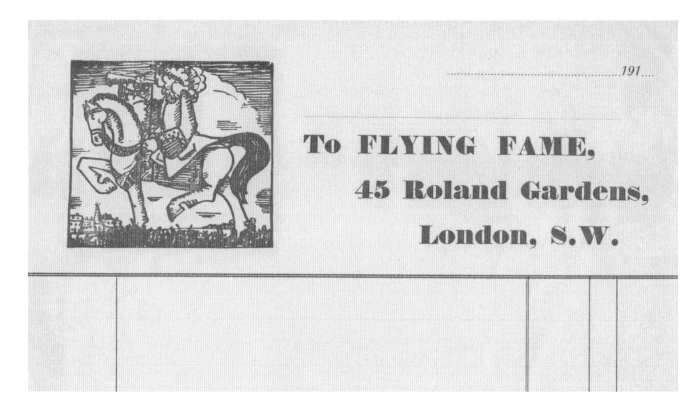

side, with writings on particular Presses, as the Curwen and Oxford University, and two major works *The Printing of Books* and *The Aesthetics of Printing.* For a very short time, before WW1, he had actually run a short-lived press with the artist Claud Lovat Fraser and the poet Ralph Hodgson, which they called The Flying Fame Press.

In *The Printing of Books* Jackson laid down his thinking on the role of printing:

> Good printing is readable printing, and no print is readable that is not simple, direct, plain and inclined towards austerity. Printing is not a thing in itself like a picture, admitting the maximum of personal expression, but part of a tool called a book; a bridge between writer and reader. It should contain nothing to impede the traffic. Self-effacement is the etiquette of the good printer.

And further:

> If at any time the printer asserts himself at the expense of the reader, becomes puffed up with pride at his own artistry so that his work struts between what the author has written and what the reader would read, he must be put back into his proper place.

A.J.A. Symonds reviewing the book in the journal *Signature* in 1938 wrote of Holbrook Jackson:

> …champion and representative of the ordinary intelligent reader, of the men with well-lined shelves and a permanent

Opposite: Ephemera from The Flying Flame Press, a short-lived press run with Claud Lovat Fraser and Ralph Hodgson.

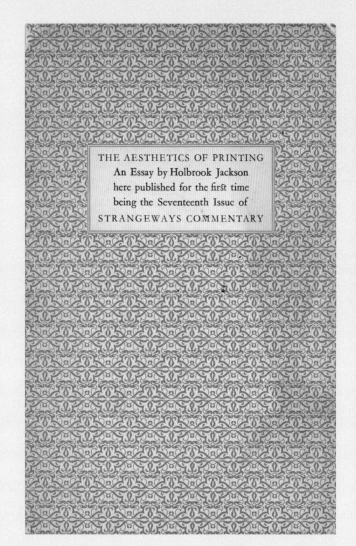

THE AESTHETICS OF PRINTING
An Essay by Holbrook Jackson
here published for the first time
being the Seventeenth Issue of
STRANGEWAYS COMMENTARY

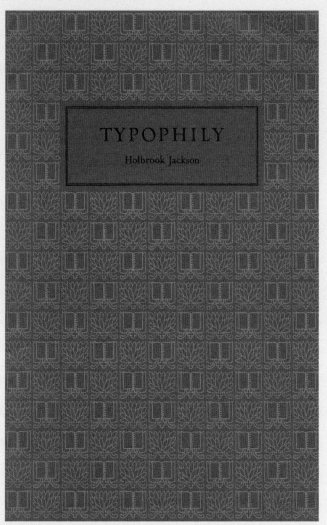

TYPOPHILY

Holbrook Jackson

curiosity concerning whatever had been printed on any press, in any type.

In his *The Aesthetics of Printing* he continued his theme of simplicity; he wanted printing to be seen as an art, as book-binding had always been, but placed himself somewhere between the excesses of the private presses and the puritanism of typographic utilitarianism; his concern all along was for the reader:

> …[of fine press books] the more beautiful they became as 'fine arts' the less useful they were for reading.

And:

> No typographer should try to add beauty to a piece of printing. Beauty should grow out of his materials and not be stuck on as an afterthought.

Yet he was concerned that printers understood and used aesthetics, but took a middle way, producing works of 'grace and charm' so long as they did not interfere with the purpose i.e. reading. He venerated the actual typeface itself as well as how it was used:

> You can read history in type-faces alone, and it may be discovered that printing types are a key to the understanding of cultural and even racial types.

Holbrook Jackson was to call his collecting of interesting examples of type 'typographic adventures'; and the love of printing for its own sake 'Typophilia'. This, in his mind was not just about books –

Opposite, left: Front cover of *The Aesthetics of Printing,* an essay by Holbrook Jackson.

Opposite, right: Front cover of *Typophily,* by Holbrook Jackson.

...not about books alone... but part of a realm which includes chapbooks and lectern Bibles, tram tickets and posters, and the infinitude of ephemera created by the jobbing printer. He [the Typophile] will assemble printed specimen books, histories of typography, treatises showing the descent of printing from script or letters carved in stone; he will be curious about the scholarship of printing, the theories and opinions of typographers, the confessions of printers, what triumphs and failures they have had, what difficulties they have surmounted, and how they have squared technique and vision.

In this he was clearly describing his own obsession with printing and with related books and ephemera.

Besides his contribution to the improving of printing by his writing Jackson was instrumental in getting similarly interested parties to join together in the common cause. When Oliver Simon conceived of a publishing society, aiming to produce one book a year to demonstrate that machine produced books could be as beautiful as hand-made ones, such was Jackson's reputation by then that he was included in a meeting along with Stanley Morison, Francis Meynell and Bernard Newdigate to discuss the feasibility of this.

Although when the Double Crown Club finally got established the drive had largely been by Simon and his friend Hubert

Foss, it was Holbrook Jackson who was to be the Club's first President and, over the years, occasionally its Secretary, and for some time its Dinner Secretary. In 1935 he wrote *The Early History of the Double Crown Club*; and, on its twenty-first anniversary in 1946, for his services, he was presented with a red Moroccan box in which he could keep his Double Crown Club dinner menus (each dinner have one designed by a member).

Holbrook Jackson rated himself a typophile, which he defined as:

> ...[he] who loves a fair page for its own sake, who regards typography as the ritual of literature, and who is exalted by the beauty of print...

Of his time he can be remembered as one of the arch Typophiles. A memorial catalogue of his own collection is held in the Special Collection section of Leeds University Library.

J.H. Mason

educator

1875–1951

I n 1936 one, J.H. Mason, was the first printer to receive the title 'Royal Designer of Industry' (RDI), an award proffered from that year onwards by the Royal Society of Arts. Mason wrote of the award:

> Such recognition of design should bring about a raised status of the designer generally, and especially of the typographic designer, which should encourage those whose bent leads them to take it up as a career.

L.T. Owens, Mason's biographer, wrote of the key role he played in the revitalizing of British printing:

> ...he achieved the dual distinction of an immediate influence on the printing of his day, and at the same time, ensuring the future of the craft he loved through the influence he had on so many of the hundreds of young people who passed through his hands.

Many of these 'young people' in their turn became lecturers and Principals of printing schools and departments across Britain, and so his influence cascaded down.

Mason was born in Lambeth and lived nearly all his life in London, his childhood spent around the Wandsworth Road. He came from a modest family, his father a coach builder. Being

Photograph of J.H. Mason taken in 1925.

relatively aimless when he left school he initially worked for a local wholesale stationer. After drifting through several more jobs Mason replied to an advertisement for a 'reader's boy' on the London site of the Scottish Ballantyne Press. Mason does not seem to have had a particular interest in printing at the time, but more in reading and in words. He later recalled:

> I early had a taste for linguistics and always wanted to read great literature in its own tongue wherein it was writ, and to this end I have made a study of many languages both European and Oriental, ancient and modern, not with the aim of mastering them, but to be able to read in them and to print them with knowledge and feeling.

It says much for Mason's strong motivation for self-education that he explored every avenue he could – evening classes, a course at University College, private tuition. The languages he was said to have acquired included Arabic, Coptic, Persian and Chinese. This early interest was to prove useful at Ballantyne's, particularly when manuscripts had to be deciphered. It was at Ballantyne's that Mason received his basic printing training, and he only left, or was obliged to leave, at the age of twenty five, when a fire at the Press left him jobless.

It was then that Mason had his first experience of private presses when, on a recommendation from one of his tutors, he was taken on at the Dove Press, which had recently been started by T.J. Cobden-Sanderson and Emery Walker at Hammersmith. Walker, a barrister by profession, from his own enthusiasm had learnt typography, engraving, and book-binding to such a level that some suggested that the whole revival of printing in Britain sprung from him. Mason came to rate the typographic work of the Dove Press, including its own Dove type, as 'unapproached' by any other. Although Mason had been stimulated by working at Ballantyne's, at the Dove Press he considered he had found 'beauty'. He wrote of the Press having: 'a real atmosphere of exaltation, as though we were concerned with some high service'.

Mason was to spend some ten years at the Dove Press, from 1900 to 1910. He felt that there he had learned a disciplined simplicity from Cobden-Sanderson as they worked closely together on a number of projects, including the Cambridge University Press bible. And, as at Ballantyne's he was called upon to help with language snags. Noel Rooke, to be a colleague at the Central School of Arts and Crafts, in 1931 recorded Mason's time at the Dove Press comparing it to the result of a severely short-sighted man getting glasses:

> So, also, Walker and Cobden-Sanderson revealed to him whole constellations of new heavens in printing, and of the literature it had come into existence to serve. Soon nothing in printing short of the best that could exist, would satisfy him.

Mason began teaching printing at the Central School of Arts & Crafts in 1905. The School by then had adopted a more 'vocational' than 'arty' stance, its early Principal, W.R. Lethaby, determined to encourage 'the industrial application of decorative art'. Cobden-Sanderson and Walker were keen that printing classes should be offered there and it was on their recommendation that Mason started to run evening classes. By 1909 he had been persuaded to work full-time and the Day Technical School of Book Production was established. By then Mason had become evangelical on the subject:

> I wish to give him [the would-be young printer] a love for, and a delight in, his trade as a means of self-expression and as a joyous activity.

Mason had a number of bees in his bonnet. He wanted his students to understand the whole process, even if they were eventually only to work on a specific aspect, so that they could fully understand and be proud of their contribution. He wanted them to catch the same pleasure from work that he did:

> The idea of printing a certain book arouses high and pleasurable excitement – it is almost like falling in love, with all the delighted service and bringing of presents, and decoration, illustration and fine garments of hand-made paper binding.

And he was determined that his students should understand what 'excellence' involved. Owens, Mason's biographer, wrote of this aspect of his approach:

> …the slightest suggestion of incipient negligence towards a struggle for excellence was instantly thrust deep into the student's consciousness, as evidence of failure of the most complete kind.

THE PRAISE OF ATHENS

AΘHNON

ΕΠΑΙΝΟΣ

ΠEPIKΛHC

ΛEΓEI

FROM THUCYDIDES: TRANSLATION BY J. H. MASON:
PRINTED AT THE L.C.C. CENTRAL SCHOOL OF ARTS
AND CRAFTS, SOUTHAMPTON ROW, LONDON, W.C.
MCMXXVII

An example of Mason's work at Central School of Arts and Crafts.

Mason felt that learning a trade should be like a university education, but one where the learning started with doing and from that moved to the conceptual, rather than the other way round:

> …mathematics will follow on the need for calculation in the workshop or trade classroom; etymology and grammar will have their points of departure in the printer's need of correct spelling and punctuation; mechanics will be used to explain the principles and construction of the mechanism of the printing machine or the marvelous composing or type-cutting machines now to be found in almost every printing office. Chemistry will explain the nature of inks and their constituents, will unveil the mysteries of lithography and collotype; and, subordinately, Metallurgy will deal with type metal.

He felt that in learning, printing students should immediately see the relevance of what they were being taught. He was scathing of the prior education of his students, those coming straight from school: 'with the three R's there is a scant residue, of the rest almost nothing is retained'. And of his work-based students, he was critical of the narrowness of the jobs they had been set to. He wanted his students to raise their technical skills and knowledge to the highest possible level and to have a broad industrial and cultural awareness.

Mason, somewhat idealistically, some would say unrealistically, felt that calligraphy should be an essential ingredient of a printer's training; certainly, he thought, more relevant than life-drawing. He maintained, as had Newdigate, that it was only by practicing writing by hand themselves that printers could fully appreciate typefaces. Drawing from his own learning experiences,

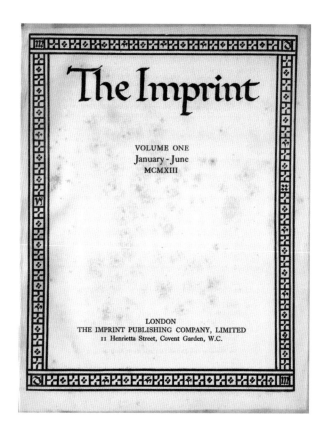

Volume One of *The Imprint* from 1913, Mason was its lettering editor.

he thought apprentices should draw inspiration from the work of the private presses. He wrote, in 1926, aims for his own printing classes:

> ...to provide not merely technical efficiency, but to embody the lessons to be drawn from research and experience of the private press, and the revival of calligraphy, and to set new standards in typography.

Mason's own personal contribution to the advancement of typography had started when he produced Imprint Old Face for the relatively short-lived journal *Imprint*. His veneration for Johnson had led him to be persuaded to become 'lettering' editor.

Imprint Old Face was said to have been the first type developed by the Lanston Monotype Company for their new compositing machine. In the *Monotype Recorder* of 1963, it was referred to as 'a typographical gem of purity and intellectual honesty': 'It was in the spirit of the Imprint that this essentially industrial design was made available to printers generally.' The *Imprint* editorial had, at the time, been more than a little self-congratulatory on its type:

> The newly designed type in which our pages are presented to the reader was cut by the Lanston Monotype Company at our instance. We are exceedingly pleased with it, and congratulate the Monotype Company at having produced the finest face that has been put on the market in modern times.

47

DIE TRAGISCHE GESCHICHTE VON
HELSINGÖR EINE TERRASSE VOR DEM SCHLOSSE.

SAXONIS GRAMMATICI
HISTORIÆ LIBER TERTIUS

HORVENDILLUS ET FENGO,
QVORUM PATER GERVEN
DILLUS, JUTORUM PRAE
FECTUS EXTITERAT EIDEM
A RORICO IN JUTIÆ PRAE
SIDIUM SUBROGANTUR.
AT HORVENDILLUS, TRIEN
NIO TYRANNIDE GESTA,
PER SUMMAM RERUM GLO
RIAM PIRATICAE INCU
BUERAT, CUM REX NOR
VAGIAE COLLERUS, OPE
RUM EJUS AC FAMAE MAG
NITUDINEM AEMULATUS
DECORUM SIBI FORE EXIS
TIMAVIT, SI TAM LATE
PATENTEM PIRATAE FUL
GOREM SUPERIOR ARMIS
OBSCURARE QVIVISSET.

Cujus classem varia fretum na-
vigatione scrutatus offendit.
Insula erat medio sita pelago,
quam piratae collatis utrin-
quesecus navigiis obtinebant.
Invitabat duces jucunda litto-
rum species, hortabatur exterior
locorum amoenitas interiora
nemorum verna perspicere lus-
tratisque saltibus secretam syl-
varum indaginem pererrare. Ubi
forte Collerum Horvendillum-
que invicem sine arbitris ob-
vios incessus reddidit. Tunc
Horvendillus prior regem per-
contari nisus, quo pugnae genere decernere libeat, praestantissimum affirmans, quod pau-
cissimorum viribus ederetur. Duellum siquidem ad capessendam fortitudinis palmam omni
certaminis genere efficacius fore, quod propria virtute subnixum, alienae manus opem
excluderet. Tam fortem juvenis sententiam admirans Collerus, cum mihi, inquit, pugnae
delectum permiseris, maxime utendum judico, quae tumultuationis expers duorum ope-
ram capit. Sane et audacior et victoriae promptior aestimatur. In hoc communis nobis
sententia est, hoc utro judicio convenimus. At quoniam exitus in dubio manet, invicem
humanitati deferendum est, nec adeo ingeniis indulgendum, ut extrema negligantur officia.
Odium in animis est; adsit tamen pietas, quae rigori demum opportuna succedat. Nam
etsi mentium nos discrimina separant, naturae tamen jura conciliant. Horum quippe con-
sortio jungimur, quantucunque animos livor dissociet. Haec itaque pietatis nobis conditio
sit, ut victum victor inferiis prosequatur. His enim suprema humanitatis officia inesse
constat, quae nemo pius abhorruit. Utraque acies id munus, rigore deposito, concordre

Bernardo Wer da?
Francisco Nein, ihr steht mir rede:
        Halt! wer seid ihr?
Bern. Lang lebe der könig!
Franc. Bernardo?
Bern. Er.
Franc. Ihr kommt gewissenhaft auf eure stunde.
Bern. Schlag zwölf. Pack dich zu bett, Francisco.
Franc. Dank für die ablösung! 's ist bitter kalt,
        Und ich bin kränklich.
Bern. War eure wache ruhig?
Franc. Alles mäusestill.
Bern. Schön, gute nacht!
        Wenn ihr auf meine wachtgefährten stoßt,
        Horatio und Marcellus, heißt sie eilen.

        Horatio und Marcellus treten auf.

4

HAMLET PRINZEN VON DÆNEMARK

Franc. Ich denk, ich höre sie. – He! halt! wer da?
Hor. Freund dieses bodens.
Mar. Und des königs lehnsmann.
Fran. Habt gute nacht!
Mar. So tretet ab, kam'rad.
        Wer hat euch abgelöst?
Fran. Bernardo steht auf posten.
        Nochmals gut nacht!
Mar. Holla, Bernardo!
Bern. Sagt, ist Horatio hier?
Hor. Ein stück von ihm.
Bern. Grüß gott, Horatio! grüß gott, Marcellus.
Hor. Nun, ging das ding auch heute wieder um?
Bern. Die wacht war ruhig, wie Francisco sagt.
Mar. Horatio glaubt an nichts, nennt birngespinst
        Das fürchterliche schreckbild, das wir sahn.
        Und darum hab ich selbst ihn hergebracht,
        Damit der augenschein ihn überzeuge
        Und seinen zweifel tilge. Mag er dann,
        Wo's wiederkehrt, mit dem gespenste reden.
Hor. Pah, pah! Es wird nicht kommen!
Bern. Setzt euch denn,
        Und lasst uns nochmals euer ohr bestürmen,
        Das so verschanzt ist gegen den bericht,
        Von dem, was wir gesehn.
Hor. Gut, sitzen wir,
        Und laßt Bernardo, was er weiß, erzählen.

LE CINQVIESME LI
VRE DES HISTOI
RES TRAGIQVES.
LE SVCCEZ & EVE
NEMENT DESQVEL
LES EST POUR LA
PLUS PART RE
CUEILLY DES CHO
SES ADVENUES DE
NOSTRE TEMPS

ET LE RESTE DES HISTOIRES ANCIENNES. LE TOUT FAICT ILLUSTRÉ ET MIS
EN ORDRE, PAR FRANÇOIS DE BELLEFOREST COMINGEOIS. A LYON PAR
BENOIST RIGAUD MDLXXXI · AVEC QVELLE RUSE AMLETH, QVI DEPUIS
FUT ROY DE DANNEMARCH, VENGEA LA MORT DE SON PÈRE HORWENDILLE,
OCCIS PAR FENGON SON FRÈRE, ET AUTRE OCCURENCE DE SON HISTOIRE.
Quoy que j'eusse deliberé des le commencement de ce mien oeuvre de ne m'esloigner, tant
peu soit, des histoires de nostre temps, y ayant assez de sujets pleins de succez tragiques, si
est-ce que partie pour ne pouvoir en discourir sans chatouiller plusieurs ausquels je ne vou-
droy desplaire, partie aussi que l'argument que j'ay en main m'a semblé digne d'estre offert à
la noblesse Françoise, pour les grandes, et gaillardes occurrences qui y sont deduites, j'ay un
peu esgaré mon cours de ce siecle, et sortant de France et pays voisins, suis allé visiter l'histoire Danoise, afin qu'elle puisse servir et d'exemple de vertu, et de contentement aux nostres,

5

An example of Mason's work for Count Kessler at Cranach Press.

48

Of even greater note was Mason's work with Count Harry Kessler's Cranach Press in Weimar. It was a recommendation by Walker to Kessler that Mason helped him in establishing the Press when everything was paused by the onset of WW1. In 1925 Kessler again contacted Mason, declaring he would 'throw it all up' if Mason couldn't help. Mason responded positively and worked with him on both the typographic and press work aspects.

In his sixties Mason reflected on what had been his aims both in his own work and in his teaching:

> To print great literature in monumental form.
>
> To study languages, including several oriental tongues, for their literature and possibilities for printers.
>
> In the Day Technical School, in accordance with the principles laid down by its founders to educate students 'in' and 'by' means of a trade.
>
> To send out a band of teachers who should carry this teaching to other centres.
>
> To raise the status of printing by making an artist of the craftsman. And teaching that that man's work should be the meaning of his life, not a means of getting a living.

An austere figure, with a forbidding exterior belying an underlying humanity and passion, Mason could be said to have gone some way towards achieving these aims; and his students did, indeed, head up other successful printing schools and by this cascade his standards and love for printing to succeeding generations.

Beatrice Warde

communicator

1900–1969

I can, I feel, be proud of 'Paul Beaujon' the scholarly writer on type-design and type-history confessing that it was reading my 'Printing for Business' in an American library that gave her her first 'slant' [as her countrymen would say] towards the craft which her intelligence now graces and benefits, and made her feel that here was work which she could reasonably devote herself to. Joseph Thorp

Beatrice Becker (Beatrice Warde as she was to become) was brought up in a one-parent family, her father, a musician having departed when she was eight. But this seems to have been no particular disadvantage to her as she had an exceptional mother, May Lambert Becker, who was to be a role model – a successful creative career woman.

May Becker, for some forty years, was a newspaper journalist, writing an advice column for the *New York Herald Tribune* and starting a weekly children's page that was rated as raising the general standard for reviewing children's books. As a role model for Beatrice she proved that a woman, sufficiently feisty, could make her way in a man's world. It was when Warde was studying at an all-female liberal arts college, Barnard College, Columbia, that she became interested in calligraphy. It is not recorded how Warde knew Bruce Rogers, the American typographer (perhaps through her mother's contacts), but it was he who provided her

Opposite: A graphic from the cover of the memorial edition of the *Monotype Recorder* dedicated to Warde, 1970.

Above: Beatrice Warde pictured with her mother May Becker.

with a letter of introduction when the library at the American Type Founders Company in New Jersey was seeking a library assistant. The Foundry possessed an outstanding library on matters relating to typography and printing, largely collected by Henry Lewis Bullen, an Australian scholar, who acted as a publicist for the Foundry. He had built up a personal library which, when merged with other collections, became the ATF Library, holding some 16,000 documents, with Bullen acting as its archivist.

Totally unqualified, but with considerable enthusiasm, good looks, and Roger's recommendation, Warde got the job, and would stay there some three years. With Bullen as her guru and open access to the books and papers, Warde had a most exceptional opportunity for self-education. Before very long she had met and married Frederick Warde, remembered as printer to Princeton University. Together they organized an exhibition 'Survivals in the Fine Art of Printing'. Among the articles exhibited were some Monotype Broadsheets of the Lanston Monotype Company in England, which were a revelation to her. In 1924 Charles Hobson, a Manchester advertising agent had started the Cloister Press, which for a time had employed Stanley Morison. Hobson was needing someone to search for good European typefaces and the Wardes were recommended (perhaps by Morison who had met Beatrice, and possibly her husband, when visiting America).

1925 saw the Wardes arrive in London. Morison, along with Francis Meynell, Holbrook Jackson, Bernard Newdigate and Oliver Simon had recently, in 1923, started a journal on typography and book design – *The Fleuron* – and Morison, knowing of Warde's

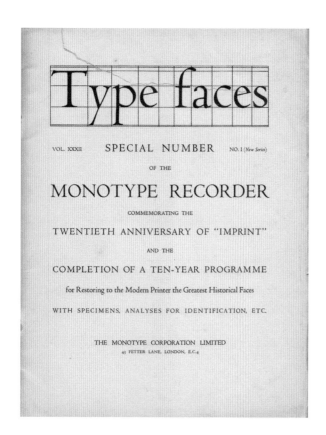

An example of the *Monotype Recorder* during Warde's reign, Spring 1933.

interests, asked her to write an article for it. Warde chose to write under a pseudonym, Paul Beaujon, as there was already a Warde, her husband, known in the world of print, but more becasuse she knew she would find difficulties making her way as a woman in a man's world, that of printing.

Her article on the Garamond types, from sixteenth and seventeenth century sources, was a work of considerable scholarship and resulted in the Lanston Monotype Company in England writing to Paul Beaujon offering 'him' a job editing its *Monotype Recorder* which the company had been issuing as part of their publicity from the turn of the century. Warde, returned to New York, accepted the offer and came back to London. Although Paul Beaujon's appearance as a woman was to surprise many, she soon showed that she was more than up to the demands of the job. It was not long before the part-time editor of the *Monotype Recorder* became the company's full-time publicity officer (referred to, in the *Penrose Annual*, as its Advertising Manager).

As Warde had feasted hungrily on Bullen's library, she was now to push to learn about every aspect of printing – mental, manual and mechanical – which she referred to as that 'which helps the printed words to leap the twelve inch chasm between the flat surface of the page and the destination in the reader's brain'. Her keenness to learn meant that she soon built the confidence and fluency to reprove typographers and printers on the errors of their ways in their own language. Typical was this comparison of Perpetua and Bodoni:

[of Perpetua] It is a light-coloured face, and photo-offset cannot in its nature add any 'colour' [thickening] during the printing; and unless the printer is a past- master the ink-prints will look, by comparison to letter-press, relatively grey or milky. The sharp thick-and-thin contrast of Bodoni could, I think, be oftener deployed to give an off-set printed page a little more snap and sparkle.

As editor of *The Monotype Recorder*, Warde was to turn a monthly publicity journal into a serious, if irregular, contributor to typographical scholarship. Further, she was to use every possible avenue to hype Monotype – visiting printing firms, giving talks, writing articles, visiting colleges. Paul Stiff described her as so full of claims for her company that she 'tried to annex the new typographic renaissance to Monotype'.

Of writing and giving talks she was to declare the former more challenging. In an interview with John Dreyfus, the book designer, in 1970, she spoke of her writing:

To me writing is the hardest job in the world – its done with sweat and agony and there is not a paragraph I have ever written which has not been re-written three or for times.

If one was to take Warde at her word she must have had a working life enduring much pain, for she was to write more than eighty articles. There could have been few publications related to printing that did not, at one time or another, carry something written either by Paul Beaujon or Beatrice Warde – trade publications as *The British Print*er and the *Printing Review*; the annuals and typographic magazines as *Penrose* and *Signature*. Such was her energy and chutzpah

Warde pictured with Stanley Morison in her garden in Surrey, 1940s.

that she even got herself featured in such unlikely publications as *The Times Literary Supplement* and *The Sunday Times*. Her name was not only attached to articles, but to forewords in books and catalogues, to reviews, and to chapters in books – all this along with her sometimes acknowledged, sometimes unacknowledged, writings for the Recorder.

What were her particular themes? Well, naturally Monotype – its machines and its type. The word 'Monotype' would appear in much of her writing, even when its relevance to the actual topic was extremely tenuous. She continued to write on type history; on the use of type for verse, Shakespeare, the Bible, newspapers whatever; on private Presses as Nonesuch; on printing apprenticeships; on the professionalism of printers; and on her two pets – Stanley Morison and Eric Gill; and the theme for which she is, perhaps, best remembered – the necessary 'invisibility' of print.

Warde was much given to metaphors, and, in 1932, when speaking to the British Society of Typographic Designers, she compared typography to a 'Crystal Goblet' – using the analogy that wine connoisseurs would prefer a clear glass to a goblet of solid gold in order to fully appreciate the contents – 'no cloud must come between your eyes and the fiery heart of the liquid'. Printed under the title 'The Crystal Goblet' along with other essays she encouraged printers:

You may spend endless years of happy experiment in designing that crystal goblet which is worthy to hold the vintage of the human mind.

Nude wood engraving of Beatrice Warde by Eric Gill, 1929.

Using a similar metaphor she was to write:

> The book typographer has the job of erecting a window between the room and that landscape which is the author's word. He may put up a stain-glass window; that is, he may use some rich superb type like text gothic that is something to be looked at, not THROUGH. Or he may work in what I call transparent or invisible typography.

Monotype, in a 'special' *Recorder* on Warde's death, wrote of her written fluency:

> What words they are: so rich and varied in colour, so logical and precise in definition, so meaningful and imaginative in metaphor. They are perfectly fitted to clothe the wealth of ideas which shot through her mind like rays of the sun, illuminating the everyday scene.

It was Monotype's custom to produce a sheet of print demonstrating each newly produced typeface and Warde responded with enthusiasm when it fell to her lot to produce one for her close friend Eric Gill's new Gills Sans. She wanted to use a text to display it that made sense 'in the smallest, grimmest or the most sophisticated of printers'. Not finding anything to meet her requirements she wrote her own. Some 6,000 copies of *This is a Printing Office* came to adorn the walls of printing offices throughout the world and even was cast in bronze and affixed to the wall of the Government Printing Office in Washington. Warde wanted every printer to have the pride of a professional, inspired by the aged Bullen's plea:

'This is a printing office' broadsheet from 1932 set in Monotype Perpetua Titling – Warde at her most evangelical.

THIS IS
A PRINTING OFFICE

CROSSROADS OF CIVILIZATION

REFUGE OF ALL THE ARTS
AGAINST THE RAVAGES OF TIME

ARMOURY OF FEARLESS TRUTH
AGAINST WHISPERING RUMOUR

INCESSANT TRUMPET OF TRADE

FROM THIS PLACE WORDS MAY FLY ABROAD
NOT TO PERISH ON WAVES OF SOUND
NOT TO VARY WITH THE WRITER'S HAND
BUT FIXED IN TIME HAVING BEEN VERIFIED IN PROOF

FRIEND YOU STAND ON SACRED GROUND

THIS IS A PRINTING OFFICE

If you're going to be just a pica-thumper, you might as well have been a plumber, they use lead to…

She wanted printers if not to practice design themselves, at least to understand its contribution, urging them to consider their trade, as she did, as at the heart of civilisation. In this vein she was to produce one of the Cambridge University Press Christmas books – *Words in their hands* with remarkable photos of printing people at work taken by Walter Nurnberg.

Wade wanted her vision to particularly influence the apprentice stage as well. She accepted that because of market pressures apprentices' day-to-day work could be restrictive, but visited many colleges to try to broaden apprentices' ambitions beyond traditional expectations.

Paul Stiff, in *Modern Typography in Britain*, derides her efforts and optimism that it was possible for a trade to reform itself by including an element of design, and, perhaps, in hindsight, his cynicism has been proved right. He considers her to have been too 'nervous' when it came to accepting European 'modernist' typography which she saw as 'aggressively original' and 'jarringly unfamiliar' and, indeed, too political – 'too concerned with Marxism synthesis'. She stood for what she termed 'new traditionalism'.

Warde was to get bored with the frustrated efforts made by some members to get her evangelism accepted into the all-male 'officer's mess' of printing and publishing – the Double Crown Club – for her evangelism. She was actually allowed, somewhat grudgingly, to speak there of Morison's achievements as a memorial offering. It was eventually agreed that she might become an 'honorary' member, but she died before this could be acted upon.

HERE WE HAVE BUILT

A SCHOOL OF PRINTING

WITHIN THESE STRONG WALLS

THERE SHALL BE TIME TO THINK

TIME TO LEARN

TIME TO PERFECT INVALUABLE SKILLS

AND TO EXPLORE NEW TECHNICS

ACROSS THIS THRESHOLD

YOUNG MEN SHALL CONFIDENTLY STRIDE

TO MEET THE CHALLENGING YEARS AHEAD

ARMED WITH SOUND TRAINING

STRANGER, BID THEM GODSPEED

ALONG THAT SUNLIT ROAD

PAUSE STRANGER: YOU STAND IN A

COMPOSING ROOM

HERE METAL STAMPS CALLED TYPES

ARE ASSEMBLED BY SKILFUL HANDS

INTO THE MASTER-PATTERNS

FROM WHICH THE VISIBLE WORD IS MULTIPLIED

FIVE CENTURIES AGO

THE INVENTION OF MOVABLE TYPE

OPENED A NEW EPOCH IN HUMAN HISTORY

BY RELEASING THE COMMON PEOPLE

FROM THE THRALDOM OF ILLITERACY

AND SETTING THEIR FEET UPON THE ROAD

TO SELF-GOVERNMENT

YOU WHO TRAVEL THAT HIGH ROAD

TOUCH NOT WITHOUT REVERENCE

THESE LEADEN SYMBOLS OF YOUR FREEDOM

REMEMBER YOUR INCALCULABLE DEBT

TO THE COMPOSITOR

WHOSE PATIENT, NIMBLE FINGERS BUILT FOR YOU

LETTER UPON LETTER

A THOUSAND STAIRWAYS TO THE STARS

'MONOTYPE' POLIPHILUS SERIES 170 & 230   16 POINT COMPOSITION & 24 POINT DISPLAY

Warde's evangelism for apprentices. An inscription from 1958 set in Monotype Castellar.

An inscription to display the capitals of Monotype Poliphilus – all were targets for Warde's mission.

Warde knew how she was seen, and indeed, how she saw herself:

> I have never ceased to be an American citizen in a foreign country. I have never ceased to be a woman in a man's chosen profession.

Monotype, in its tribute to her on her death, entitled an issue of *The Monotype Recorder* 'I am a communicator'. And that was what she was, both in her extensive and extraordinary writing and in her electric speechifying – her fluency enhanced both by her relaxed informal style and her attractive appearance. To what extent she managed to advance her evangelical goals is questionable, but she certainly cannot be criticised for making anything less than an all-out effort to spur the indifferent and lethargic along the way.

Harry
Carter

archivist   1901–1982

He remains one of the least-known best-known men in the world of books. He has chosen nearly always to be an accompanist, a Gerald Moore, rather than the soloist he could be. Francis Meynell

Harry Carter, born into a middle class family, grew up around the Croydon area, south of London. The family appears to have been comfortably off, having live-in servants and able to send their children to private boarding schools. His father was the headmaster of a London school and was, himself, talented, combining an interest in languages with practical skills. That Bedales was chosen as a secondary school for Carter, says much for the interests and liberal values of his parents for it was what in those days was termed 'progressive' in that it put as much emphasis on practical, social and survival skills, as on academic ones.

Carter, encouraged by his father, became something of a linguist by the time he reached his teens, competent not only in Greek and Latin which he had started in preparatory school, but in Spanish, French and German as well; and he was already putting pen to paper in his contributions to the Bedales' newspaper.

Harry Carter at his bench.

From Bedales, Carter got a scholarship to read history at Queen's College, Oxford. Little is recorded of his time there, or, indeed, of his subsequent career path into law, articled to a solicitor in Lincoln's Inn and called to the bar in 1925. And, curiously, there is no account for his sudden passion for printing and his sudden major switching of career. What is known is that within a year or two after qualifying for the law he had his own small press and type at home and had begun to attend classes on engraving at the Central School of Arts and Crafts and to receive some tutoring at a foundry for punch-cutting.

Carter had been friends with John Rothenstein, a fellow Bedales' student, and through him with his cousin, Oliver Simon. Whether this friendship had triggered his interest in print is not clear, but by 1928 Carter was providing patterned papers for Simon's employer, the Curwen Press, and experimenting with a new type that the Curwen was using, Lutetia, And it was while he was still a lawyer that Carter accompanied Simon, in 1928, on a 'printing' tour of Belgium and Holland which included visits to the Plantin-Moretus Museum, the Amsterdam Type Foundry, Enshede en Zonen printers in Haarlem and various paper mills.

It was not long before Carter, inspired by Stanley Morison, got himself a 'learners' job in the Monotype Corporation, for which Morison was design adviser. Although a 'learner', Carter was able to contribute to new type design, but, of greater significance, began to work on what was to be his first major publication, a translation of Fournier's *Manuel Typographique* of 1764.

Carter moved on to become assistant works manager for the Kynoch Press in Birmingham. Caroline Archer in her history of the Press referred to Carter's time there as 'productive'. Initially he reported to Herbert Simon, Oliver's brother, an inspiring manager.

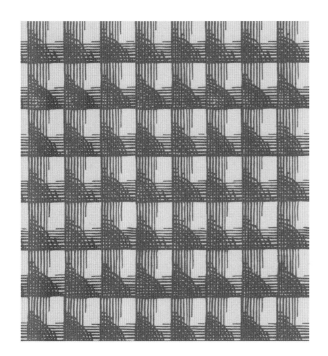

An endpaper pattern created by Carter for the Curwen Press.

In such an encouraging environment Carter not only worked on books but designed both a Hebrew and a Russian type.

He also produced type specimen books, using Ravilious woodcuts and having covers with raised lettering, which were considered 'a breath of fresh air, whetting the appetite of the typographic connoisseur'. He was also to work on the Kynoch Press Notebooks and Diaries, sent out to friends and clients at Christmas, serving both as goodwill gifts and publicity. And, with Herbert Simon, Carter co-authored, in 1931, a practical handbook for schools and interested amateurs, *Printing Explained*, which Francis Meynell claimed was the first practical book on the subject for over a century.

The Kynoch work environment became altogether less stimulating for Carter when Simon left in 1933, and a new manager arrived who had been the Press' commercial manager and accountant; altogether less inspiring and, in this case, less efficient. For Carter it became something of an uphill struggle even to get new type bought and in 1936, when the situation had become intolerable for him, he resigned.

It was during the Kynoch Press period that Carter was also working out his ideas on types and printing by writing articles for a number of newspapers and professional journals, including the *The Sunday Times*, *The Observer*, *Signature* and *Typography*. And it was while he was at the Press that he completed his translation of Fournier, printed at the Curwen Press, his first significant publication.

From the Kynoch Press Carter moved on to work as production manager at the Nonesuch Press of Francis Meynell, which by then had been taken over by George Macey of the Limited Editions Club, Meynell remaining as designer on a part-time basis. Meynell wrote of Carter's time there:

> [Carter] was my Nonesuch understudy; sometimes indeed my overstudy. It was he, not I, who chose the typeface for the Dickens and persuaded the Monotype Corporation to produce it. He found the brilliant illustrator, Michael Ferrier, for the Comus, and made the typographical researches, and then the map, for White's Selborne.

The twenty-four volume Dickens was well-received with many press accolades as 'the most glorious achievement of publishing in our time'. And Carter's work on *The Mask of Comus* was rated as 'the most beautiful of all books printed in the Fell type'. However, Nonesuch began to lose money and Carter, who had had difficulties with Macey, was asked to leave. Then, thirty-eight, with wife and child, Carter filled his time with some teaching at the Central School of Arts and Crafts and some bread-and-butter commissions for catalogues and advertisements; and then war was declared.

Carter, with his language skills, was taken into the Postal and Telegraph Censorship organization; and by 1941, he found himself out in Palestine as Deputy Chief Censor. Later he was transferred to Bucharest as Censorship Adviser to the British Military Mission, returning to Palestine in 1945 as Chief Censor. In the midst of all this, Carter took delight in creating some Hebrew punches for a bible and some for local printers.

Working Party Reports

JEWELLERY AND SILVERWARE

LONDON: H.M. STATIONERY OFFICE

1946

PRICE 3s. 0d. NET

To the President of the Board of Trade

Sir,

We, the members of the Jewellery and Silverware Working Party, which was appointed by you in March, 1946, have examined to the best of our ability the matters remitted to us in accordance with our terms of reference, and we now submit our report.

In general we have been able to base our conclusions less upon statistical evidence and published material than we should have liked to do ; but we have been fortunate in receiving the greatest possible help in verbal testimony from a considerable variety of witnesses with wide knowledge of the trade. Even so, we have been forced to give many of our conclusions in general terms, and in some aspects to confine ourselves to urging the need for investigations and planning which, if fuller documentation had been available, we might have hoped to perform ourselves in the time allotted to us. This circumstance has naturally affected the general form of our recommendations.

We are convinced that the industry with which we were charged to concern ourselves is to-day, as it was in its earliest times, one industry, and that it is vital to its welfare in the coming years that it should regard itself, and be regarded by the Government, as one industry. It contains within itself, however, a wide variety of manufactures, and we ask the indulgence of those who know the trade if we have from time to time in the wording of our report inadvertently spoken as if a particular conclusion or comment, which has an intimate bearing on a particular section, had a more general application to the industry as a whole than in fact it has. We have been on our guard in this matter, and have tried neither to be misled ourselves nor to mislead others.

We owe our warmest thanks to the many individuals who have helped us generously with their evidence and suggestions, and to those who welcomed and instructed us in their factories. We particularly wish to record our gratitude to those friends of the British industry in the United States of America and in France, who did so much to make the visits of our missions to their countries extremely pleasant to the delegates personally as well as helpful in high degree to the work of the Working Party ; and in this connection we should like especially to mention the names of Mr. Edward J. Otis, of The New England Jewellers' Association, Providence, R.I., Mr. W. R. Howell of the Commercial Department, British Consulate-General, New York, and M. Maynier, Vice-President, La Chambre Syndicale de la Bijouterie Jouaillerie et Orfévrerie. We also wish to thank the Prime Warden and the Wardens of the Worshipful Company of Goldsmiths for their hospitality to us at Goldsmiths' Hall on many occasions when we have met in London.

We also desire to put on record our indebtedness to our Secretary, Mr. W. O. Newsam, and our Assistant Secretary, Miss Ockenden. Mr. Newsam has used all his great energy and tact in turning our Working Party into a going

In 1946 the Government, at the suggestion of Francis Meynell, set up a design office within Her Majesty's Stationery Office (HMSO). HMSO was an enormous organization with four printing sites in and around London, as well as commissioning work from commercial printers, which, for one reason or another, that they could not do themselves. Its task was to handle the printing of all government and parliamentary papers, ceremonial scripts and the likes, as well as acting as a jobbing printer for whatever the needs of the various government departments; the heavy load of the daily issuing of Hansard took precedence.

Government printing had never been at the caprice of royalty, as it had been on the Continent. Carter put it that the British Government felt it should publish, that it was generally for giving information and against secrecy, but that it had never felt any obligation to publish well. There had been a report, in 1922, 'on the best faces of type and modes of display for Government printing', that resulted in the general use of Old Style, with Caslon Old Face for covers and titles preferred, but that was about it. It was perhaps the outstanding standard of the Ministry of Information output, during the war, with Edwin Emberton running its printing arm, (which Carter was to rate as 'faultless'), that stirred the Government to take a fresh look at how it was doing when it came to printing in peacetime.

With Meynell now in charge, albeit on a part-time basis, he set about what he considered his first task – to bring in 'the right man' to run his new design unit. Having worked with Carter at Nonesuch and, presumably, impressed with Carter's record since that time, he was the chosen one. With Meynell as, 'honorary' typographic adviser at HMSO having numerous other commitments he needed someone solid to run the unit. Meynell described his own contribution as 'snatching a few half hours for ceremonial jobs'; and described Carter as his 'executive brain and hand'.

The situation Carter faced was running a body, controlled by the Treasury, with a vast throughput, a slightly reluctant Government, and definitely reluctant Government departments with his aim being to try to improve standards. Arthur Phillips, who worked with Carter at the time, described the situation: 'the staff was competent and did nothing to browbeat a department to accept avant garde design at the whim of a typographer'.

In that, at this time, Carter was writing and speechifying on Government printing, with articles in *The Penrose Annual* and *Alphabet & Image*, and an after-dinner talk at the DCC, it was as if by doing such he could work out what his strategy might be back at base. He was finding the Government barely open to good design, let alone to invention or experimentation. One catches something of his up-hill battle with a description he gave of his relationship with the Meteorological Office:

> I tried to exclude all funny type. I can never see a bold without regret. Attempts to wean the Met. Office of Old Style with Clarendon, have been repulsed, but I managed to get a new heading for the Monthly Weather Report...

Carter made what changes he could to get not only optimum legibility but to attain some satisfactory middle position between 'over-design and quackery' and 'dullness and uniformity'. He was able eventually to build a team of some seven men for the Design Unit, which came to be known as Carter's Circus.

Ruari McLean, an admirer of Carter, wrote enthusiastically: 'Harry Carter is gradually making official publications look as if

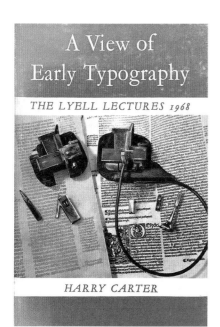

The front cover for the first edition of Carter's book *A View of Early Typography*, 1968.

they had been written by, and for, human beings'. Carter, valiantly, continued the battling for some six years or so, describing his move to the Oxford University Press as an 'escape'. Morison was to write of Carter:

> Carter is versatile and able, but it seems to me that he has never made his mind up to be absolutely thorough in the exercise of his many talents, with the consequence that from an employer's point of view he is somewhat distant and inconstant.

Certainly Carter's leaving of jobs seems sometimes to have been on a sour note, albeit he, himself, might have justified the leaving as a matter of principle, of standards. In spite of Morison's somewhat tetchy summary of Carter's career, it was he who recommended Carter to Charles Batey, the Printer at the Oxford University Press:

> Harry Carter possesses a combination of talent that, without any exaggeration, ranks as unique in the English trade. At least I know of no-one else in this country who is comparable with Van Krimpen and Conrad Bauer for knowledge of type design and type production and with the history of these techniques and associated crafts; he also possesses a wide knowledge of process.

It was at the Oxford University Press (OUP) that Carter was to have the most productive and satisfying period of his working life; he had found his niche. Now well into his 50s, he not only systematically organized its typographic assets, acting as its archivist, but carried out much of the research drudgery for Morison's book on

Fell, and set to work on organizing the considerable typographic material held at the Plantin-Moretus Museum in Antwerp.

At OUP he not only worked at cataloguing but put on exhibitions, organized visits to the Press, researched OUP's paper mill, made translations, researched for future books and even, himself, developed a type for some of the Press' religious productions. And more, for in addition to his work in Amsterdam, Carter spent time in Edinburgh helping to catalogue the Edward Clark Collection, held at the Heriot-Watt College, which consisted of some five thousand items related to typography and the development of printing from the fifteenth century.

In the extensive bibliography of Carter's writings given in The Old School Press's *Harry Carter, Typographer*, there are some seventy titles dated for the years before he joined OUP, and well over a hundred for during his time there.

Carter, once committed to a project, worked with great intensity and speed, using both brain and hands. An example is when Morison asked him to help mount an historical exhibition on typography in London, Carter not only wrote on typography for the catalogue, selected the punch-cutting equipment to be displayed, but actually demonstrated punch-cutting during the exhibition.

Along with his many projects at the Oxford University Press Carter was active at the DCC. He had been elected as a member in 1932, was, for a time, its secretary, and became President in 1951. He was also to give a few after-dinner talks to members even before becoming a member, with one talk on type founding in 1930; later he was to talk on a subject related to his work at OUP, on the influence of Dutch printing on Oxford printing. And in his late 60s, in the position of the James P.R. Lyell Reader in Bibliography at Oxford University he gave five lectures on printing type and their history, by then he was one of the most knowledgeable on the subject in Britain.

Perhaps considered one of Carter's major achievements was his first volume of *A History of the Oxford University Press to the year 1780*, which was published in 1975. A further volume was started but Carter was getting progressively ill with Parkinson's Disease, retiring from the Press in 1980 and dying in 1982.

Carter was a linguist, translator, archivist, writer, designer, punch cutter, printer – yet a man of modesty. Martyn Thomas, in an article in Matrix 31, rated Carter above Morison in that he had such hands on experience as well as written skills, and recommended the reader to read anything by Carter that they could find:

> I ought to say that among writers on type and printing for whom I have special regard – and I am not the only one – is Harry Carter. This is because his writing has exceptional clarity and brevity. But chiefly because he had a special qualification for writing about punch-cutting and printing at the hand press. I have done a few of these things. Unlike Updike and Morison, Carter had done them all.

Brooke Crutchley

moderniser

1907–2003

When a tribute to Brooke Crutchley was produced in book form on his retirement from the University Press at Cambridge in 1974, those contributing included the Chief Scientific Adviser to the Government, the President of the Publishers' Association, and even a trade unionist, the General President of the National Graphical Association, such was the spread of his influence and his capacity for friendship.

Born into a middle class family and raised in Bedford Park, a then fashionable new housing development beyond Hammersmith, Crutchley was educated away from the area, in a preparatory boarding school and then on to Shrewsbury. Gifted academically, he got a scholarship to Trinity Hall, Cambridge, where he read classics for two years and English in his last year.

At university he was involved in student publications, with both *Granta* and *The Cambridge Review* and seemed all set for a career in journalism. Between his schooling and university he had had a trial run at the *Yorkshire Post*, and, finishing his degree, he returned there as a sub-editor. However, by then, this appears to have been a fallback choice for he had actually applied to the University Press but had been turned down. However, there must have been something about his application that had impressed the then printer to the University, Walter Lewis, for he later wrote to Crutchley offering him an interview which resulted in him, a relatively raw youth of twenty three, with little knowledge of printing, becoming Lewis's assistant. Lewis is said to have declared 'I want

Photograph of Brooke Crutchley, 1953.

someone who doesn't know anything so I can teach him myself'. As it turned out Lewis did relatively little in that respect.

Crutchley's father was to be employed by one organization all his working life – the Civil Service – and Crutchley was to repeat that pattern. But whereas his father had had to slog his way up the many rungs of the Civil Service, Crutchley only had to take one step to get the top post of Printer to Cambridge University when Lewis retired in 1945. Crutchley was to spend some forty-four years with the University Press, twenty-eight of them as its printer. This could suggest that he had got himself a cushy number and, avoiding trouble, stayed the course. But Crutchley was anything but a time-server; he was a reformer, an initiator, a persistent change agent, a smoother of feathers here, an encourager there – handling each challenge diplomatically and modestly. In the retirement tribute he was described as 'a man of intellect, charm, steadfast consistency of purpose and unimpeachable integrity'. A non-printer in charge of a major Press he was to become an influential figure, not only in Cambridge, but nationally.

Lewis had been the university printer since 1923, and with his dynamic energy had done much to up-date the equipment, enlarge the premises, and it was he that brought in Stanley Morison as adviser. He had had a solid technical basis behind him as general manager of the Ballantyne Press and then working with Charles Hobson's Cloister Press. Crutchley was left to pick up what technical know-how as he could, learning much from Morison and from visits to paper mills, binderies, and such. Relying on his brainpower

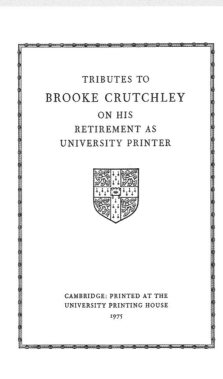

Above: Title page of the book, *Tributes to Brooke Crutchley*, published on the anniversary of his retirement, 1975.

Right: The front cover design for Crutchley's book, *To be a printer*, published by The Bodley Head, 1980.

BROOKE
CRUTCHLEY

To be a printer

**THE UNIVERSITY PRESS
CAMBRIDGE**

The University Printer
[WALTER LEWIS]
is always ready to give
estimates for the printing
of literary and scientific
works demanding high
standards of proof-reading
and typography

Cructchley saw printing as a matter of 'intellectual engineering not of pyrotechnics' and that seems to have got him through. Although Crutchley was to write an account of his working life in Cambridge (*To be a Printer*), because he tended without false modesty, to use the pronoun 'we' rather than 'I', it is not always easy to disentangle his personal contribution. There is evidence of printing going on at Cambridge University from the sixteenth century, when it received its charter to print from Henry VIII. Although, initially, the Press operated relatively independently, the University gradually took over, setting up a Syndicate to control the operation of its Press. By the time Crutchley arrived the Syndicate consisted of fourteen members, with the University's Vice-Chancellor and Treasurer as ex officio members. The Press had only become a publishing house as well as a printer towards the end of the nineteenth century. Crutchley was to inherit both the historic reputation of the Press and the distinguished one of Walter Lewis.

His first significant venture was just before the onset of the war when he instigated a mammoth exhibition to celebrate the quincentenary of Gutenberg:

Our intention was not to follow the customary line of portraying printing as an art but rather to demonstrate its social applications and the benefits it had brought to various fields of human activity.

It was a considerable project, for which Beatrice Warde was drawn in to help organize. It unfortunately ran for

Opposite: Publicity for The University Press, from *Signature* 1939.

Right: View of the courtyard of the University Press, Cambridge.

little more than a week, having to be closed because of the possibility of air raids ahead. After a spell at the Admiralty during the war, Crutchley returned to the Press, now in the role of printer, with the challenge of revitalizing the Press in a time of austerity and rationing yet with a considerable backlog of work piling up.

Consequently his first concern was output; he wanted a higher production rate, yet with costs cut and deliveries quicker. His was one of the first printing firms to bring in work study and payment by results. Crutchley managed this smoothly and with his employees' full commitment; the industry took notice. From then on he built up a consultative operation with sectional representative committees, and employee job satisfaction a continual concern. One example of his sensitivity to his staff was his demarcation of the role of designer in order to leave creative scope for the compositor:

> We made a point at Cambridge of confining the designer's
> role to setting the framework, leaving the compositors to

Flow diagram of the new printing-house at Cambridge University Press, 1962.

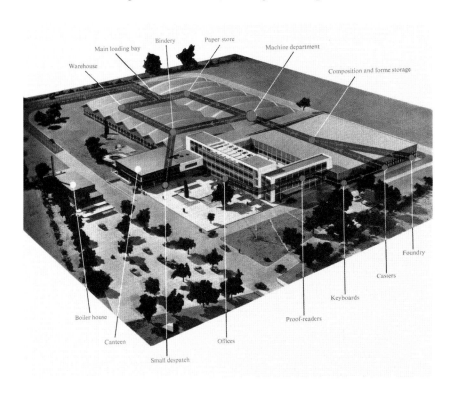

use their know-how to the full. Nothing, we considered, was more frustrating for a man who had learnt a craft to find himself deprived of all initiative.

This genuine concern for employee job satisfaction can again be illustrated with the planning of a new building. The Press had outgrown its original building, and as early as 1947 Crutchley was campaigning for a new one, away from the crowded city centre. He put human factors equal to technical and commercial ones in the planning:

> All along, the inherent problems in designing an efficient printing house have been seen as psychological ones as much as mechanical – how to create the conditions in which men and women could most happily and effectively carry out their varied and often complicated tasks.

Crutchley brought in the Applied Psychology Unit of the Medical Research Council to advise on such considerations as noise, lighting, atmospheric conditions, along with such niceties as planning a courtyard so that all employees would have an outside view. He recorded:

> Employees have been kept in close touch through all stages of planning, and their ideas and views have been incorporated in the design.

It was not, actually, until 1963 that he was able to open the new University Printing House, an impressive single storey building covering some forty acres.

A PRINTER'S
CHRISTMAS BOOKS
1930–58

Crutchley can certainly be considered a pioneer of human relations in the printing industry, but he was no slouch when it came to its technology and products. From extension of the Press's type pool to major changes in its compositing, he was constantly alert to what was happening in printing both nationally and internationally. As a manager of a major Press he must have made more trips to America than any other. There would hardly have been any American University that had a Press that he did not visit and where he had not formed firm friendships. He was one of the first in Britain, if not the first to computerize compositing and his Press came to be seen as one of the most technically advanced in the country. It was said that 'the rest of the world followed suit'.

His concern for the improvement of lettering extended beyond the Works, into Cambridge itself, for he started a campaign to improve lettering in public places, particularly when it came to street names. This concern was to reach the heights of the Ministry of Transport, the Fine Art Commission and the national press. In 1977, when Crutchley received the Royal Society of Arts Bicentenary Medal the citation included:

> He has taken a particular interest of lettering in public places and it was his initiative that led to improved street name-plates after the last war.

When it came to books, journals and other printing assignments passing through the Press, Crutchley made a major change by introducing sub-editors to reduce problems and time wasted at the proofing stage. Throughput was also helped by him insisting on guiding principles for layout etc. that the Press should have house rules.

Being a University Press it had regular work dealing with such things as examination papers (hundreds of thousands) and other university requirements. Responding to the University's needs, and to those of other universities, Crutchley built up the Press's reputation for printing scientific texts, particularly exacting jobs with oftimes complex illustrations. Printing scientific texts, whether in the form of books or journals, was not a profitable business. Crutchley had got to know Lord Zuckerman, Scientific Adviser to the Government when printing a journal he was involved with, and the two of them set out to convince the right people that the printing of such was actually a matter of national importance, that the future of the country depended on scientific advances and therefore of scientific text printing. Yet again the matter reached the portals of Government with a Consultative Committee on Scientific Printing being set up hopefully to become a driving force. All this evangelism appears to have had but a marginal effect on the undertakings of other printers and Cambridge was to remain the one with an international reputation for such a speciality.

Amongst all this activity, Crutchley found time to revive a custom started by Lewis, of producing small Christmas books in limited editions for friends and clients of the Press, 'simply to give pleasure – to ourselves in the making, and to our friends in the reading'. These charming offerings came in all shapes and sizes and were issued through to his retirement in 1973. Their content was largely related to printing matters or to Cambridge itself, with such titles as 'The Survival of the Baskerville punches'. One, particularly close to Crutchley's heart was when he got the aged Stanley Morison (a godfather to one of his children) to record the tally of types that through him were cut for the Press in the 1920s.

Crutchley was also able to set time aside to put pen to paper himself with articles and books – sometimes as co-author, covering a wide range of printing subjects including a history of his own Press and biographies of his two key predecessors – Stanley Morison and Walter Lewis.

In his auto-biography Crutchley claimed to have, at one time or another, sat upon over forty committees relating to the printing industry, including the Coldstream Committee on Art Education. His considerable contributions were rewarded not only with the RSA Medal, election to Presidency of the Double Crown Club in 1952 and of the Institute of Printing (of which he was a founding member) in 1972, but with a CBE in 1954.

Robert
Harling

chinese juggler

1910–2008

Younger than Stanley Morison, Francis Meynell and Oliver Simon, Harling was a link between the old and the new generations just beginning to become designers. Ruari McLean

If Harling didn't fit in to either the earlier or the later generations of 'Printing People', it was equally difficult to allot him to one specialism or another when it came to his career – advertising executive, typeface designer, editor, consultant, author – oftimes several of these at the same time. Harling has been described as 'secretive' and certainly this applied to his upbringing for he had it that he was an orphan brought up by his 'aunt', a friend of his mother's. And certainly he did spend some time living with an 'aunt' which took him to Brighton and then back to London (where he actually had been born, his father a taxi driver). Nor can one be quite certain as to Harling's education. He attended Owen's School in Highbury, but then was rejected by Oxford, and, somewhere along the line, he appears to have taken classes at the Central School of Arts and Crafts; beyond that he seems to have learnt 'on the job'.

For a short time, he ran a bookshop in Lambs Conduit Street, but at the age of twenty-two, had his first, and possibly only, full-time employment when he joined Stuart Menzies' advertising agency in 1932. He learnt a good deal from Menzies, who had acquired such clients as Shell, Imperial Airways and Elizabeth Arden, and who Harling looked up to as 'no-one in the history of advertising had made such a killing'. Harling, at Stuart's, gained experience in the various activities of the agency, albeit Menzies, famous for his work with Fortnum & Mason, kept the copy-writing for himself. Later in his career Harling worked as Creative Director for Everett, Jones & Delamere, another agency. He described himself as coming to typography from an advertising background and therefore as much, if not more, interested in display type as that for books and journals.

By his mid-twenties, Harling had begun to focus his work interest on printing, with short spells at Lund Humphries in Bradford, and at the Kynoch Press in Birmingham. Records with Lund Humphries have him mounting an exhibition for them on

Robert Harling at John Lewis's Meadow Cottage, Woodbridge, Suffolk.

Rudolph Koch and the Klingspur Foundry in 1935, which says something for his self-confidence for his knowledge and his experience of printing would have been embryonic at the time.

The challenge with researching Harling is that frequently the dates do not tie up. But as he was wont to do three or four things at the same time this is perhaps no surprise. 1935, then, has him at Stuart's, yet mounting a Lund Humphries exhibition, writing articles on print (e,g, on Tschichold for *The Printer*), designing typeface for the Stephenson Blake Foundry and starting a print magazine *Typography* with James Shand of the Shenval Press. Of his type designs for Stephenson Blake, Harling wrote:

> I began work upon three projects with zest, discovering an unceasing delight in working within the rigid limitations imposed upon the designer by the metal and machines by which his design must ultimately be made, by the strict requirements of legibility and 'fitness for purpose'.

James Shand had started the Shenval Press in 1930 and, by the mid-1930s had brought in Harling as design adviser. It is thought that the idea of the Press publishing a journal on printing, to be called *Typography*, was Harling's; and although the first issue had Shand and Ellic Howe as co-editors with him, by the second issue Harling was its sole editor. *Typography's* prospectus announced:

> The sponsors of Typography believe that fine book production is not the only means of typographical expression or excitement. We believe, in fact, that a hand-bill can be as aesthetically pleasing as a bible, that a newspaper can be as typographically arresting as a Nonesuch. This catholicity

SUMMER 1938 · PUBLISHED QUARTERLY BY THE SHENVAL PRESS · TWO SHILLINGS

TYP
GRAPHY 6

Left: Front cover of *Typography* number 6 from the Shenval Press, Summer 1938.

Opposite: Front cover of *Alphabet and Image* number 1, produced with James Shand, 1946.

will show itself, we think, in the contents of this first issue which are outlined in this prospectus and in future issues which already engage our time and tempers.

Typography was to appear from November 1936 until the summer of 1939 – eight issues in all, presumably closing with the onset of war. True to the prospectus the first issue contained articles on Kardomah tea labels and Shell advertising. The journal attracted very varied contributors, many from outside the printing world, as

Misha Black, John Betjeman, Christian Barman and John Gloag; but a goodly crowd of designers as well, including Eric Gill, Harry Carter, Francis Meynell, Jan Tschichold along with Harling and Shand – and a mixed band of other typographers, graphic designers, academics and crusaders of design.

Harling's exploits during the war, when he met up with Ian Fleming are well-recorded elsewhere. By 1946 he was back with Shand producing a new journal *Alphabet & Image*, which again ran for eight issues, the last being for December 1948. This was quite a rash enterprise for there was still rationing of printing supplies and a general feeling of austerity. Harling, as editor yet again, used a considerable mix of contributors including Ambrose Heal, the furniture retailer (a collector of printing ephemera), old stalwarts as Francis Meynell and Stanley Morison, along with a new generation of printing people as Brooke Crutchley and Ruari McLean. Its most frequent contributor was one, A.F. Jackson, the Deputy-Keeper of Printed Books at the British Museum, expert on typography and the author of the book *Encyclopaedia of Type Faces* – a

GEORGE CRUIKSHANK

We have pleasure to announce that the first three titles in our series on English masters of black-and-white, under the general editorship

SIR JOHN TENNIEL

of Graham Reynolds of the V & A, will be published in the autumn. They will be quickly followed by titles in an INTRODUCTION TO ARCHITECTURE

AND RICHARD DOYLE

series and other books. The authors of the three books noted above are Ruari McLean, Frances Sarzano and Daria Hambourg respectively.

ART AND TECHNICS

The books will be 9 × 7 *inches in size, cloth bound, profusely illustrated*

Above: An advertisement for the Art and Technics imprint, 1947.

Opposite: Front cover of *Image* number 1 from the Shenval Press, Summer 1949.

standard on the subject. By the end of 1948 Harling's interests seemed to be shifting from printing towards art, architecture and interior design and the Shenval Press's third journal *Image*, first issued in the Spring of 1949, contained little to do with print. It came out under the Shenval Press imprint 'Art & Technics' – yet again the brainchild of Harling. The imprint was to publish some forty books including some on Harling's own personal interests in sailing and architecture.

Although Harling has been panned as 'nostalgic', 'too-damned English', and 'self-satisfied', in that part of his career when he was focused on printing, he produced new typefaces (Chisel and Playbill becoming widely used), wrote one of the first articles that was published in Britain on Jan Tschichold, mounted an exhibition on Klingspur, and was design adviser to a number of newspapers including the *News Chronicle* and *The Times*. He was well aware of Britain lagging behind Europe on typography, and deplored it. In the *Penrose Annual* of 1936 he wrote:

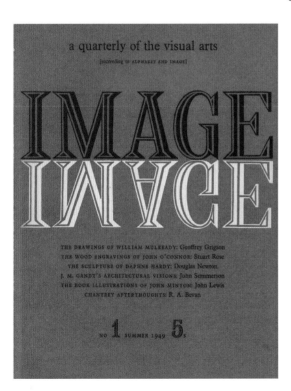

…typographically we are an unenterprising race. Almost all the display lines we see in the press and in our booklets are introduced from abroad. We seem to think that after Mr. Gill has anglicised the Sans for our weaker Anglian eye, there is no further contribution to be made to the typography of display. We go to Germany, to France, or to America and seize upon all that is fashionable in those centres.

Without formal training in typography he could write and talk on the typographic scene with the ease of someone thoroughly familiar and confident in his knowledge, and assured in his opinions. Typical was such a passage as:

> Othello as a substitute for the fierce Neuland of Rudolf Koch is ludicrous; whilst to introduce Monotype Script No. 385 into competition with foreign Script is pathetic.

When it came to contributions to printing, Harling could also be said to have been a pioneer in urging the industry to commission artists to design type. In one article he wrote:

> One day I shall compile a list of these men [potential artist/ typographers] and give it to the waiting world with some erudite title as; 'Check-list of letter forms designed by several English artists of note, considered uninteresting by the latter-day English type-founder and composing machine maker.

He defended the apparent parochialism of the journals he had edited as although knowledgeable and admiring of much of what was going on abroad, he felt it his mission to promote the many unknowns operating in Britain.

By the mid-1950s Harling had drifted from his intense activity related to printing to other areas of design. For some twenty six years, from 1957, he was the titular editor of *House & Garden*, his name added to those of Leonie Heighton and John Bridges for the plethora of coffee table books it produced; and this alongside his becoming architectural correspondent for *The Sunday Times*, and even trying his hand at novel writing; a Chinese juggler to the end.

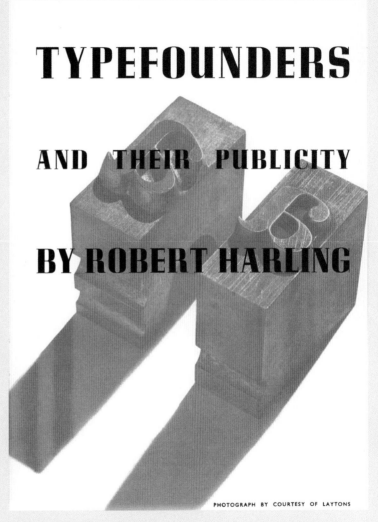

Above: Front cover of *Image* number 3 from the Shenval Press, Winter 1949–50.

Right: *Typefounders and their publicity* by Harling.

Epilogue

We have entered a new typographic era and the commercial printer having learnt his lesson from the amateur is now producing books which would be distinguished even amongst the masterpieces of the past.

Holbrook Jackson, 1938

By now the reader will have come to appreciate the complex macramé of some of the key players in the revival of British printing in the twentieth century – who influenced who, who mentored who, who worked in collaboration with who, who met at the Design & Industries Association events, ate together at the Double Crown Club, who wrote about who – a vast industry, a rich knotting of key players.

These 'Printing People' were passionate; their lives can be described as love stories. Beatrice Warde would tease her audiences with talk of her love affairs (with all aspects of print); the stoney-faced Mason compared even the suggestion that he was going to be asked to work on a certain book as 'almost like falling in love'; Holbrook Jackson wrote of the love for certain specifics in printing: 'as lovers augment passion by idealizing some detached feature or possession of the loved one'. Thorp wrote of striving for perfection:

> ...this quest for beauty is a species of lunacy... but it is in
> the same divine succession of lunacies as love...

If a helicopter, aerial-view, of British typography and printing in the twentieth century is taken, possibly these players can be described as 'small fry' – largely parochial, offering only a traditional kind of modernism. Perhaps it was the next generation of Jesse Collins at the Central School, Herbert Spencer at the Royal

College, or even the noisy, brassy, political, colourful generation after them, that brought about the real renaissance.

But, in their modest contributions, in their different roles, these Printing People, prodded indifferent business men; widened the horizons of technical colleges and art schools; got rid of the excesses of the Victorians and Edwardians; encouraged the foundries; stirred the traditionalism of printing organisations; even challenged Government practice. It could well be claimed that these underrated enthusiasts were to till and fertilise the unpromising soil without which the courage and éclat of their successors might not have been so successful.

Bibliography

Joseph Thorp, *Printing for Business*, John Hogg.

Joseph Thorp (ed.), *Design in Modern Printing: The year book of the Design & Industries Association, 1927–28*, Ernest Benn Ltd.

T (of Punch), *Friends and Adventures*, Jonathan Cape.

Holbrook Jackson, *The Printing of Books*, Cassell & Co.

Bernard H. Newdigate, *The Art of the Book*, The Studio Ltd.

Joseph Thorp, *B.H. Newdigate, Scholar-Printer*, Basil Blackwell.

Ruari McLean, *Modern Book Design*, British Council.

Holbrook Jackson, *Typophily*, North-Western Polytechnic.

Beatrice Warde (comm.), *Words in Their Hands*, Cambridge University Press.

'I am a communicator', *The Monotype Recorder*, vol 44, no.1.

James Moran, *Stanley Morison*, Lund Humphries.

Francis Meynell, *My Lives*, Random House.

Herbert Simon, *Song and Words*, George Allen & Unwin.

'Tributes to Brooke Crutchley', Cambridge University Press.

L.T. Owens, *J.H. Mason 1875–1951*, Frederick Muller Ltd.

Brooke Crutchley, *To be a Printer*, The Bodley Head.

Sebastian Carter, *Twentieth Century Type Designers*, Lund Humphries.

John Lewis, *Such Things Happen*, Unicorn Press.

Ruari McLean, *True to Type*, Oak Knoll Press.

Caroline Archer, *The Kynoch Press*, The British Library / Oak Knoll Press.

Martyn Thomas et al., *Harry Carter: Typographer*, The Old School Press.

Paul Stiff (ed.), *Modern Typography in Britain*, Hyphen Press

Numerous articles from the journals: *The Penrose Annual*, *The Monotype Recorder*, *Signature*, *Typography*, *Art & Image* and *Image*.

Appendix

Some contributors to the British printing renaissance in the first half of the twentieth century.

A few of these have had books written about them or have written autobiographies; many at least have had articles about them; a few just remain footnotes awaiting a fuller recognition.

Harry Carter

Brooke Crutchley

Harold Curwen

R.B. Fishenden

William Gamble

Eric Gill

Eric (Peter) Gregory

Thomas Griffitts

Robert Harling

Ellic Howe

Frederick A. Horn

Edward Humphries

Eric Humphries

A.F. Jackson

Holbrooke Jackson

Edward Johnston

John Lewis

Walter Lewis

J.H. Mason

Francis Meynell

Gerard Meynell

Stanley Morison

Bernard Newdigate

Fred Phillips

James Shand

Herbert Simon

Oliver Simon

Vincent Steer

Joseph Thorp

Emery Walker

Beatrice Warde